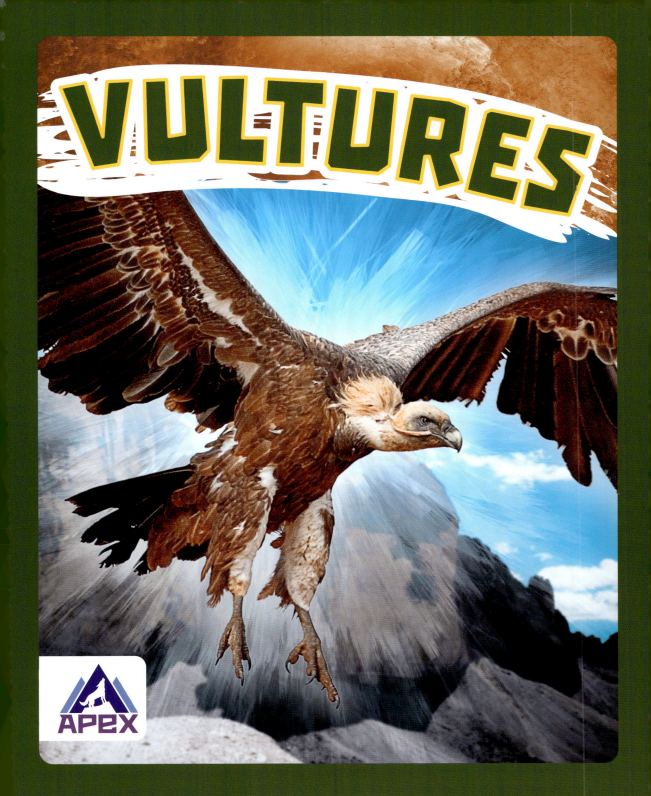

VULTURES

BY MEGAN GENDELL

WWW.APEXEDITIONS.COM

Copyright © 2022 by Apex Editions, Mendota Heights, MN 55120. All rights reserved. No part of this book may be reproduced or utilized in any form or by any means without written permission from the publisher.

Apex is distributed by North Star Editions:
sales@northstareditions.com | 888-417-0195

Produced for Apex by Red Line Editorial.

Photographs ©: Shutterstock Images, cover (bird), 1 (bird), 4–5, 6–7, 8, 9, 10–11, 12–13, 14–15, 16–17, 18–19, 20, 21, 22–23, 24–25, 26, 27, 29; Unsplash, cover (background), 1 (background)

Library of Congress Control Number: 2021915671

ISBN
978-1-63738-148-9 (hardcover)
978-1-63738-184-7 (paperback)
978-1-63738-255-4 (ebook pdf)
978-1-63738-220-2 (hosted ebook)

Printed in the United States of America
Mankato, MN
012022

NOTE TO PARENTS AND EDUCATORS

Apex books are designed to build literacy skills in striving readers. Exciting, high-interest content attracts and holds readers' attention. The text is carefully leveled to allow students to achieve success quickly. Additional features, such as bolded glossary words for difficult terms, help build comprehension.

TABLE OF CONTENTS

CHAPTER 1
FINDERS KEEPERS 5

CHAPTER 2
BIG BIRDS 11

CHAPTER 3
FINDING FOOD 17

CHAPTER 4
LIFE IN THE WILD 23

Comprehension Questions • 28

Glossary • 30

To Learn More • 31

About the Author • 31

Index • 32

CHAPTER 1

FINDERS KEEPERS

A turkey vulture flies above the trees. She can't see the forest floor. But she smells something. It's a dead fish.

Turkey vultures are known for their bright-red, bald heads.

The vulture flies down to the fish. She uses her sharp beak to tear the meat. Then she gulps each piece down.

A vulture's beak can rip muscle and skin. Some vultures can even break bones!

A turkey vulture can smell a dead animal from more than 1 mile (1.6 km) away.

Soon, two smaller vultures land near her. They want to eat, too. They chase the first vulture away.

Vultures often fight one another for food.

Some vultures throw up at other animals. They do this to scare the animals away.

TOO MUCH FOOD

Sometimes vultures eat too much food. They become too heavy to fly. So, they throw up some of the food. This makes them comfortable enough to fly away.

CHAPTER 2

BIG BIRDS

There are 23 types of vultures. These large birds live all over the world. Most vultures live in open areas. In those places, it's easier to find food.

Many vultures live in grassy fields. They can also be found near mountains or forests.

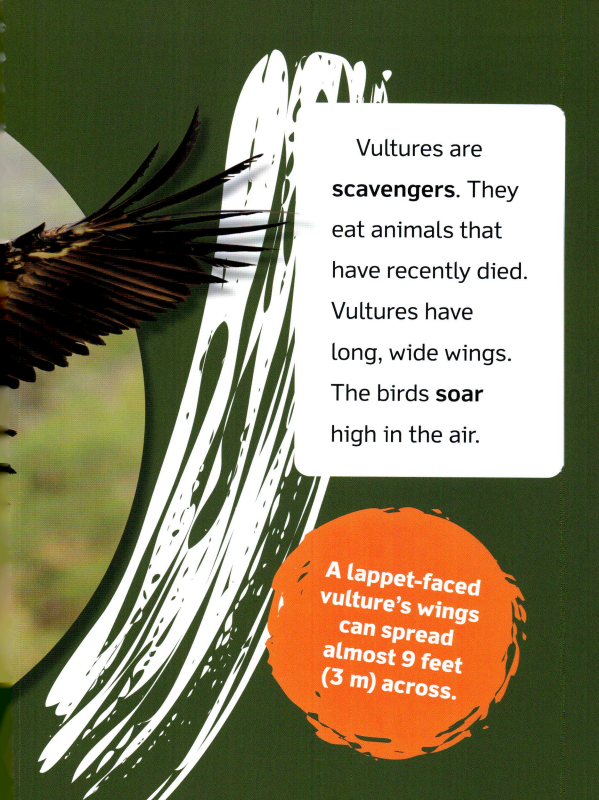

Vultures are **scavengers**. They eat animals that have recently died. Vultures have long, wide wings. The birds **soar** high in the air.

A lappet-faced vulture's wings can spread almost 9 feet (3 m) across.

Vultures have hooked beaks. The beaks' sharp edges tear food. Many vultures have few or no feathers on their heads and necks.

STAYING CLEAN

When a vulture eats, it sticks its head into a dead animal's body. Feathers might get covered in blood. A bald head is easier to keep clean.

A hooded vulture has a partly bald head.

CHAPTER 3

FINDING FOOD

Vultures spend lots of time flying and searching for food. Some vultures use their strong sense of smell. Others rely on their eyes.

Vultures can soar for hours. They often fly in circles.

When one vulture flies down to eat, other vultures might notice. They descend, too. They may join from miles away.

The bearded vulture eats mainly bones.

Several vultures often eat the same animal. Some even work together to find food.

The vultures take turns eating. The biggest and strongest go first. But groups of other vultures sometimes chase them away.

Vultures may return to the same dead animal for days to keep eating.

Some vultures pee on their feet. This helps cool their feet. It also helps kill **germs**.

White-backed vultures live in Africa. People often hunt and kill these birds.

DANGEROUS FOOD

Humans use some chemicals that are poisonous to vultures. These chemicals can get inside animal **carcasses**. Vultures that eat them will die. Some vultures have even become **endangered**.

CHAPTER 4

LIFE IN THE WILD

Vultures often **roost** in groups. They sit together on cliffs, in trees, or on the ground.

A group of griffon vultures rest in trees in Spain.

Some vultures make nests in groups, too. Others **breed** in pairs. Some vultures build nests from sticks. Others use small **hollows** in trees or rocks. Most vultures lay one or two eggs at a time.

Egyptian vultures lay eggs on rocks. These birds usually live alone or in pairs.

A young vulture's parents feed and protect it.

Both parents sit on the eggs. After one or two months, the eggs hatch. About nine weeks later, the babies can fly away. However, they often stay with their families.

STOPPING DISEASE

Rotting animals can spread diseases to people and other animals. But vultures can eat them without getting sick. By eating dead animals, vultures help keep diseases from spreading.

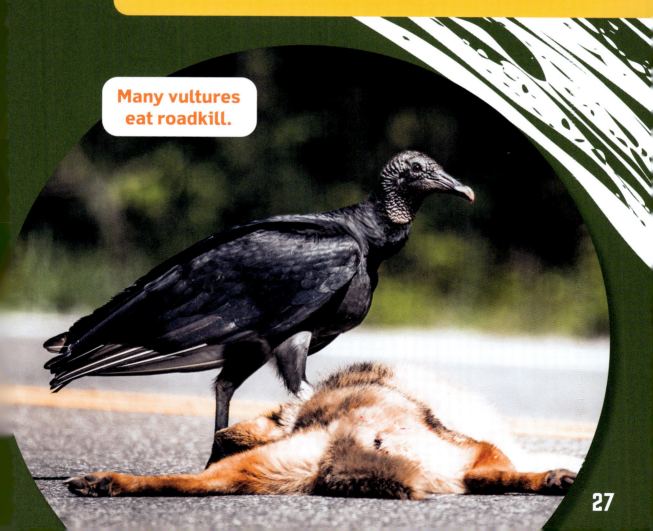

Many vultures eat roadkill.

COMPREHENSION QUESTIONS

Write your answers on a separate piece of paper.

1. Write a few sentences describing the main ideas of Chapter 3.

2. Vultures can live alone, in pairs, or in large groups. Do you prefer being by yourself or with others?

3. How many eggs do most vultures lay at a time?

   A. just 1 or 2
   B. about 23
   C. more than 300

4. Why would it be easier for a vulture to look for food in an open area?

   A. There is more grass for the vulture to eat.
   B. There is more sunshine to keep the vulture warm.
   C. There are no trees to block the vulture's view.

5. What does **bald** mean in this book?

*Feathers might get covered in blood. A **bald** head is easier to keep clean.*

    A. full of hair or feathers
    B. having no hair or feathers
    C. brightly colored

6. What does **descend** mean in this book?

*When one vulture flies down to eat, other vultures might notice. They **descend**, too.*

    A. to fly down
    B. to run away
    C. to make loud sounds

Answer key on page 32.

GLOSSARY

breed
To come together to have babies.

carcasses
The bodies of dead animals.

colonies
Groups of animals that live together.

endangered
In danger of dying out forever.

germs
Tiny living things that can cause illness.

hollows
Empty spaces or holes.

roost
To rest or sleep.

rotting
Falling apart after dying.

scavengers
Animals that eat dead animals they did not kill.

soar
To fly high in the air without flapping wings very often.

TO LEARN MORE

BOOKS

Hamilton, S. L. *Vultures*. Minneapolis: Abdo Publishing, 2018.

Levy, Janey. *The Bizarre California Condor*. New York: Gareth Stevens Publishing, 2020.

Sommer, Nathan. *Vultures*. Minneapolis: Bellwether Media, 2019.

ONLINE RESOURCES

Visit **www.apexeditions.com** to find links and resources related to this title.

ABOUT THE AUTHOR

Megan Gendell is a writer and editor. She lives in Vermont. She likes to take long walks and watch birds fly above mountaintops.

INDEX

B
babies, 26
beaks, 6, 14
bearded vulture, 19
breed, 24

C
cliffs, 23

D
dead animals, 7,
13–14, 21, 27

E
eggs, 24, 26

F
food, 9, 11, 14, 17

L
lappet-faced
vulture, 13

N
nests, 24–25

R
roosting, 23

S
scavengers, 13
smell, 5, 7, 17
soaring, 13

T
trees, 5, 23–24
turkey vulture, 5, 7

W
wings, 13

Answer Key:
1. Answers will vary; **2.** Answers will vary; **3.** A; **4.** C; **5.** B; **6.** A